FRANZ SCHUBERT
and his Merry Friends

BY OPAL WHEELER AND SYBIL DEUCHER

ILLUSTRATED BY MARY GREENWALT

Franz Schubert and His Merry Friends
Written by Opal Wheeler and Sybil Deucher

ISBN 978-1-933573-13-7
Published January, 2008
Printed in the United States of America

Zeezok Publishing, LLC
PO Box 1960 • Elyria, OH 44036
info@Zeezok.com

www.Zeezok.com

FRANZ SCHUBERT
and his Merry Friends

MUSIC

CHAPTER ONE

THE CHILL WIND swept down the chimney and rattled the doors and windows of Schoolmaster Schubert's house on the street called "The Gate of Heaven," just outside Vienna. Over the doorway hung the sign, "The Red Crab," that creaked and swung on its rusty hinges.

It was cold and draughty on the second floor of the old house, for Schoolmaster Schubert earned little money teaching the boys in the Lichtenthal school and found it difficult to buy enough fuel to keep his family warm.

Early on this bitter January day a little boy was born in the Schubert home. His father carefully laid him in the low cradle that he had made of rough pieces of pine wood and pulled it close to the clay hearth, where his new son would be snug and warm.

The very next day the new baby was carried to the parish church nearby and christened Franz Peter Schubert.

The winter was long and hard but little Franzl grew rapidly and before he could talk or even stand on his short chubby legs, he sang sweetly and clearly.

Every evening he waited for his father's footsteps to sound on the outside stairs for then there would be music, after Mother Schubert had given them their evening meal.

But Franzl cared little about his supper and would sing loudly, beating time on the table with his spoon.

"Hush, little one," said his mother. "It is not yet time for music. You must be patient until your father is ready to play."

His brothers, Ignaz and Ferdinand, watched with delight as the little brother waved his arms in time to his singing.

"Listen to our Franzl, good wife — already he sings real tunes," said Schoolmaster Schubert. "Some day we may have a singer in our household, Elizabeth."

Father Schubert took his instrument from the tall cupboard and soon the deep tones of his cello and the high clear notes of Ignaz's violin sounded through the house. Little Franzl sat on the floor close by, bending and swaying to the music.

"Our small son enjoys the evening concerts," said Father Schubert, putting down his bow.

"Yes, Theodor — I never saw such a child!" answered Mother Schubert from her high-backed chair where she sat busily mending. "He sings from morning until night and seems to care for nothing else."

It was not long before Franz Peter picked out tunes for himself on the old worn-out hackbrett, or piano. He made up little exercises and played them over and over, his dark curly head bent closely over the keys.

Franz Peter could not see very well even though he wore thick steel-rimmed glasses every day. Many times he would stumble and fall when he played games with his merry friends. He wished that he did not have to wear the spectacles and could see as clearly as other boys.

Someone was always calling:

"Your glasses, Franz — you have forgotten them!"

Near the Schubert home was a large factory where pianos were made and Franz Peter went there with his cousin as often as his mother would allow him.

The two boys eagerly watched the different parts of the instruments as they were fitted together and then hurried to the warehouse where the shiny new pianos stood waiting to be sold.

They rushed from one instrument to another and climbed on the high stools to play on the polished keys. Franz picked out little tunes and taught them to his cousin, his short stubby fingers running swiftly over the keys.

"Now you play on the high notes of another piano while I stay here and play the piece on the low keys — then it will sound like a duet!" cried Franz, his dark eyes shining behind his steel-rimmed glasses.

The boys played on and on, shrieking with delight, and ran from one piano to another to try out the tone of the different instruments.

It was cold in the factory but they would not leave until it became too dark to see the keys.

In the evening, after Schoolmaster Schubert came home from his day's work, he gave Franz lessons on the violin and before long he was able to play easy duets with his father.

His brother Ignaz helped him with the piano and in a short time Franz went far beyond his older brother.

"Now you can go on alone for you have learned all that I have to teach you," said Ignaz.

Father Schubert called his family earlier than usual on Sunday mornings for he wanted everyone to be on time for the services in the parish church of Lichtenthal.

Franz Peter sat next to his father and was quiet as long as there was music. When it was over he became restless and the hard bench was very uncomfortable.

"Be quiet, Franz! You must sit still and listen to the service."

"But I would rather sing in the choir with the boys," whispered Franz.

"Perhaps later we shall speak to the director. But now you must be patient until the service is over."

There stood Michael Holzer, the fat, jolly choirmaster in his long robes, directing the small orchestra and the singers.

When the organ sounded its last notes and the people were leaving the church, Franz and his father went to find the choir leader.

"Good day, Herr Holzer. I have brought my young Franz to see you. He thinks he would like to sing in your choir."

"Indeed!" said the director, looking down at the small, dark-skinned boy. "He looks a little young, but we will see what he can do."

"You will find that he reads his notes well and that his time is good," said Father Schubert. "His brother Ignaz and I have taught him music at home."

Herr Holzer opened a large book to a difficult song. Franz sang it so easily that before he had finished, the director turned to the schoolmaster.

"But, my good friend — why have you not brought this boy to me sooner? He has a fine voice indeed. Of course he must have more training, so he shall come to me at once for lessons."

"Then will I sing in the choir with the other boys?" asked Franz, eagerly.

"First you must learn more about singing, so tomorrow you will come here and we will begin to work," said the choirmaster.

The next day Michael Holzer was surprised to find that his pupil knew so much about music. And now Franz worked very hard and in a few weeks he was happy to be singing with the boys on Sunday mornings, high in the choir loft.

There were lessons on the organ and on the piano, too. But most of all, Herr Holzer was delighted when his pupil was able to make beautiful compositions from little melodies or themes that he played for him.

One afternoon Schoolmaster Schubert came to see the choirmaster.

"And how does the music go with my young Franz, Herr Holzer?"

"Ah, my good Schubert, I have never had such a pupil! Whenever I bring him anything new, I find that he already knows it!"

"Then do you think that he would be able to enter the court choir school in Vienna?"

"That is hard to say, my friend, for even though Franz has a fine voice, there is little chance of his being taken into the Convict. Only eighteen boys are admitted and there are always many waiting to join."

"But just today I have heard that there is a place for one boy. Franz would learn other things besides music and that would be well, indeed, for some day he must become a schoolmaster, like all the Schuberts."

"It is said to be the finest school in Vienna, with the greatest masters in all the city," answered Holzer.

"Many times I have tried to enter Franz there so that we would have one less to provide for in our home. It would mean much to have him live at the Convict where he would be clothed and fed as well."

"Then surely it would do no harm, Herr Schubert, to have Franz try the examinations, but we cannot expect that he will be chosen when there are so many who are anxious to enter."

It was late in the evening when Theodor Schubert reached the small courtyard and climbed the stairs to his home on the second floor

"Well, Franz — you will go to Vienna with me in the morning to try the examinations at the Convict."

"To sing before the music masters?" cried Franz eagerly.

"Yes, and we must start early for there will be many waiting to enter the court school."

Mother Schubert came quickly into the room.

"Then at last there is a place for a new choir boy, Theodor?"

"Just one — and we all hope that Franz will be chosen."

Mother Schubert hurried about, brushing and cleaning the coarse rough clothes that her son was to wear to the royal choir school. His suit had worn very thin and she worked late into the night patching the ragged coat.

Early the next morning Franz and his father walked through the old streets of Vienna under the bright yellow trees that glowed in the October sunshine.

When they came to the entrance of the Convict, they made their way into the dimly lighted hallway where boys were already seated on long benches, waiting to try the examinations.

Franz sat near the door in his old homespun suit, his spectacles sitting firmly on his short, stubby nose. He listened anxiously for his name to be called.

At last after many hours, a voice sounded through the long corridor.

"Franz Peter Schubert — from the district of Lichtenthal!"

Franz sprang up quickly and as he hurried through the long line of boys there was a burst of laughter at his coarse gray suit and shabby hat.

"See the miller's son in his dusty clothes! And how will the miller sing?" they whispered laughingly to one another.

But Franz pretended not to hear them and went quickly down the long room to the chapel where the masters were waiting.

He was given one difficult question after another.

"Ah — here is a boy who knows much about music," said Master Eibler to Salieri. "And now we must hear him sing."

When the high clear voice of Franz Peter rang through the long chapel, the boys sat up and listened in wonder.

The masters were amazed and delighted. Never before had they heard such beautiful singing in the Convict.

When the song was finished, they talked quietly together. Franz stood waiting, his old worn hat held tightly in his hand. He watched anxiously as Herr Körner, the singing master, walked slowly through the chapel and called in a loud clear voice:

"The examinations are over. Franz Peter Schubert will put on the court uniform for he has been chosen the new member of the royal choir school!"

Franz was too excited to speak. He went with the master to a room where he quickly put on the splendid uniform — a dark brown coat with gold border, bright polished buttons, and a gold epaulette on the left shoulder. There was a fine long waistcoat, knee breeches, and shoes with shining buckles.

Last of all, he put on the low three-cornered hat and went to find his father.

"Surely this cannot be my son!" exclaimed Schoolmaster Schubert delightedly, as he looked at Franz in the bright costume. "Come — we must hurry home to tell your mother and brothers of the good fortune that has come to you!"

They walked out into the late afternoon sunshine and were soon climbing the stairs to the Schubert home.

Everyone crowded around to see the beautiful uniform.

"Now I am to live at the royal school and tomorrow I will begin to work there with the masters!" cried Franz.

"You will leave us so soon?" said his mother as she hurried to put steaming bowls of food on the table. "Then come and we will have our evening meal so that there will be time for some music with your father and brothers."

Franz sat at the long table and while his brothers looked admiringly at the new costume, he told of the examinations and singing before the masters.

Theodor Schubert went to get his cello while Ignaz and Ferdinand tuned their violins. Franz took his viola that he had just learned to play and soon the music of an old quartet sounded through the house.

Everyone in the Schubert household was up early the next morning. Franz stood in his shining uniform, ready to leave for the royal choir school.

"Ah, my young Franz Peter, how we shall miss you!" said his mother, sadly.

"But I will come home on Sunday afternoons and on holidays, too," answered Franz quickly.

"It is time we were off for Vienna!" called his father from the open doorway.

They went down the narrow stairs to the small courtyard below and walked quickly toward the city.

The sun was not yet high when they came to the old worn steps of the Convict. Franz said good-bye to his Father and as he went into the dark gloomy building he wondered if he would like his new home.

CHAPTER TWO

CHAPTER TWO

A LOUD BELL sounded through the cold dark halls of the Convict each morning, long before the sun came to light the old streets of Vienna.

Franz Peter shivered as he crept out of bed onto the stone floor for there was no heat in his small bare room.

Quickly dressing himself, he hurried down the draughty halls with the other boys to eat the small bowls of porridge. Now there would be eight long hours to wait until time for the last meal of the day.

It was difficult for Franz to study the lessons in reading, geography, and arithmetic through the long morning hours for he was always hungry. He bent over the desk, his spectacles close to the study book, for it was dark in the chill room with only a dim light coming through the high narrow windows.

When the afternoon lessons in history, poetry, French, and Italian were over, it was time for singing and Franz was happy again.

It was not long before he was playing in the band and singing in the royal chapel choir.

Franz liked the jolly master, Herr Ruziczka, who played the viola in the court theater and taught the boys the violin and the piano at the Convict.

"I did not know that you could play so well, Franz. You must join the school orchestra at once. At first you will start with the second violins and if you work hard enough, some day you will play with the first violins."

The next day it was time for Franz to begin his duties in the orchestra. He hurried about, placing music on the stands, tuning the instruments, and putting fresh candles in the waxy iron holders so that there would be enough light to read the music.

When he had finished his tasks, he went to his place in the second row and eagerly waited for the director to begin the rehearsal.

"There is not enough music for everyone, Franz, so you will read from the score of Spaun, in front of you. Now we will begin with the symphony of Haydn."

Herr Ruziczka gave the signal and the music began. Franz was overjoyed to hear the merry melodies of the great composer, Joseph Haydn, who was an old man and lived in a little house not far away.

Franz liked to listen to all of the instruments sounding together. He played his part joyously and the tone that came from his violin was clear and true.

When the first part of the music was over, Spaun turned quickly to see who was playing with such smooth tone and without making any mistakes.

"You must be the new boy who has come to live with us. What is your name?"

"Franz Peter Schubert."

"Well, Franz," laughed Spaun, "you play much better than I who have been in the orchestra for many years. I suppose you will become a musician some day?"

"Oh, no — my father would never allow me to do that. He does not want me to spend too much time with music."

They began to play again and when the symphony was over, the boys went to the dark cold study rooms to prepare their lessons for the next day.

Often when they finished their studies they wanted Franz to join them in their games, but he hurried off to find a quiet place where he could write down all of the music that poured into his mind each day.

Even at night when everyone was asleep, he would light the small candle beside his bed and soon the scratching of his pen sounded through the small room as he wrote his melodies.

Sometimes he would stop to listen to the songs and laughter of the happy people of Vienna as they danced and sang along the narrow streets far into the morning. Then he would take the small pieces of paper that were filled with his merry tunes and put them carefully away before going to bed.

This jolly melody that he wrote is called a rondo. It is part of a sonata. Can you play it?

RONDO
(MUSIC APPRECIATION DISC 5 TRACK 43)

Franz worked hard at his studies every day and Theodor Schubert was glad to have the good reports that the masters sent to him of his son's work at the Convict.

One morning Franz Peter tried again and again to prepare his lessons but melodies kept running through his mind and at last he closed his book and began to write.

Faster and faster went the notes on the paper and soon there was no more space. He looked eagerly about for more paper but there was none to be found.

Close by was a small table covered with a white cloth. Yes — that would do! Franz ran to it and in a short time it, too, was almost covered with notes that became smaller and smaller to save room. He bent closer over the cloth to see his work.

"Whatever are you doing, my young friend?" asked a friendly voice. "A musical tablecloth, indeed!"

Franz sat up suddenly and found Spaun looking down at his work.

"Why — you see — I could not find enough music paper for this melody and I had to finish it," said Franz.

"You write music?" asked the older boy, kindly.

"Sometimes — when I can find paper. But there is never enough to write all of my melodies."

"Come now, and play this music that you have written, so that we can hear how it sounds."

Franz went to the piano and without looking at the music, played it exactly as he had written it.

Spaun listened closely and then began to walk excitedly about the room.

"But, Franz — this is beautiful music! You must be sure to write every melody that comes into your mind!"

"There would never be enough music paper to do that, for my people are very poor and they could not send it to me."

"That is easy," laughed Spaun. "I have some money of my own and I will see that you have all of the music paper that you can use."

"You are very kind, indeed!" cried Franz, his eyes shining. "But I fear that my father would be very angry if he knew that I spent so much time in writing music."

Franz liked to write songs. This beautiful lullaby of his you will enjoy singing.

CRADLE SONG
(MUSIC APPRECIATION DISC 5 TRACK 44)

peace-ful be thy dream-ing, While she rocks thee

in thy cra - dle bed.

Franz was happy to be at home on Sunday afternoons for then there were concerts with his father and brothers. Often he wrote little songs and quartets for them.

As they played the new music, his brothers sometimes made mistakes.

"No, no, Ferdinand — it does not go that way. Now then, let me show you," cried Franz eagerly, and taking the violin, he played the difficult part correctly.

His father, too, often made mistakes and when Franz's quick ears heard them the first time, he said nothing. But when the same mistakes were played again, he said gently:

"There must be something wrong somewhere, Father."

"Wrong? But where could it be wrong?"

"I think I can find it," said Franz quietly, pointing to the place in the music.

They liked to listen to Franz's waltzes. He wrote many of them and they are such fun to play.

WALTZ
(MUSIC APPRECIATION DISC 5 TRACK 45)

Herr Lange, the director of the Convict, was very stern and became angry if the boys did not know their lessons.

Franz found it difficult to add figures in arithmetic and trace mountains and rivers on the map of the world, for he was always hearing music. He sat chewing his pen and drummed little tunes on the work table with his short stubby fingers.

When he could stand it no longer, he closed his book quietly, took paper from his pocket and forgetting everything around him, began to write his melodies. There was enough music paper now, thanks to his good friend Spaun.

The boys as well as the masters were very fond of Franz Peter for he was always a good-natured, jolly companion.

"Franz! Franz! Where are you?" called loud voices outside the window one afternoon. "Come out with us! We need you!"

There was no answer, for Franz had not even heard them. His head was bent closely over his work and notes were coming from his pen as fast as he could write.

"Franz Peter Schubert!" called the stern voice of the director, who sat nearby and noticed the music paper in front of his pupil. "We will have no composing in study hours!"

"Yes, sir," answered Franz, quickly putting the new music out of sight.

In the evening, when his lessons for the next day were finished, Franz stole quietly to the music room. Mozart was one of his favorite composers and he sat at the piano to play one of the master's sonatas.

When he had finished he looked up and saw that someone was sitting in a corner of the room.

"Spaun! I did not know that you were here!"

"I was enjoying your music, Franz. But a Mozart sonata — is it not difficult?"

"Yes, Mozart's music is difficult to play well — but it is so very beautiful!" and turning again to the piano, he began to go over the parts that he liked most of all.

Suddenly he stopped playing and began to hum a melody of his own. He tried it first with one hand and soon both hands were flying over the keys in a merry dance.

Almost at once there was the sound of moving feet and voices humming the melody. Franz looked up to see Spaun and his friends Stadler, Senn, and Holzapfel merrily dancing and singing about the room.

"Bravo! Bravo, Schubert!" they cried, ending the dance with loud stamping of feet.

"Spaun tells us that this is your music, Franz!" cried Senn. "Did you really write it yourself?"

"It is nothing — really nothing at all," answered Franz quietly.

"Play it again!" exclaimed Stadler, pounding Franz on the back. "Play it, Schubert!"

"No — not that one. You will like this one better!" cried Franz. Then another melody rang through the room, and shouting merrily, the boys began to dance again.

Suddenly the music stopped. There in the doorway stood the angry Herr Lange.

"What is the meaning of this confusion?" he cried.

Spaun faced the director.

"We asked young Schubert to play for us, sir, and I suppose we became a bit noisy."

"Schubert was playing his own compositions for us," added Senn. "Come, Franz — play the dance again for Herr Lange."

Franz turned quickly to the piano and started a new dance, making up the music as he went along.

As he played, Herr Lange began to smile, and when the dance grew merrier still, he nodded his head in time to the music.

"Well, my young Schubert," said the director when Franz had finished, "so you compose music! Then we must have our great master Salieri see your work. And Herr Ruziczka has been telling me that you do well on the violin, too."

"I like music — more than anything else, sir."

"Music is all very well, young man, but see that you do not neglect your studies."

He turned to the boys.

"Now then, you have made enough noise for one night. It is time that you were all in bed," said the director as he left the room.

This music that Franz wrote makes us want to dance, too.

GERMAN DANCE
(MUSIC APPRECIATION DISC 5 TRACK 46)

Franz was sad indeed when the day came for his friend Spaun to leave the Convict. He had received training to become a lawyer in return for his services in the chapel choir and was now ready to earn his living in the city of Vienna.

"What shall I do without you, Spaun?" said Franz. "No one cares as much about my music as you."

"But I will come back often to play and sing," answered Spaun kindly. "And you will have new music for me to hear each time that I return."

Franz missed his good friend and now he worked harder than ever at his studies. Theodor Schubert had been well pleased with his son's work at the Convict for these past two years.

But soon it became more and more difficult for Franz to find time to prepare his lessons, for he was always needed for special rehearsals.

"Come, Schubert," called Herr Körner, his short pigtail bobbing up and down as he spoke. "You are the only boy who can sing the solo parts in the service on Sunday, so you must rehearse with me now."

Franz was excused from his lessons and followed the short, thin little master into the chapel, where he sang until he was breathless.

On other days he was needed for extra rehearsals of the orchestra and so at the end of a few weeks he discovered that he was far behind the other boys in his lessons, for there had been no time to prepare them.

One bright Sunday afternoon he left the choir school and started for his home. In his pocket was a new quartet that he had written the night before. He was happy, thinking how pleased Ferdinand would be, and hummed the melody as he climbed the stairs to his home.

When he reached the top, the door opened suddenly and there stood Theodor Schubert, angrily shaking a letter at Franz.

"You have brought shame upon the name of Schubert by neglecting your lessons for music! From now on you shall not enter this house until good reports of your work come to me again!" cried his father, and quickly shut the door.

For a moment Franz did not move. Then he started slowly down the stairs and for many hours wandered about the streets of Vienna.

It was late when he found himself at the entrance of the Convict. He went inside the cold gloomy building and on down the long dark hall to his room and crept into bed.

You will want to listen to this beautiful impromptu that Franz Schubert wrote.

IMPROMPTU
(MUSIC APPRECIATION DISC 5 TRACK 47)

CHAPTER THREE

CHAPTER THREE

24th November, 1812

Dear Ferdinand,

I have been thinking much about my life here and find that it is good on the whole, but in some ways it could be much better. You know that one can often enjoy eating a roll and an apple or two, especially after having nothing for eight and one half hours, and then only a little supper to look forward to. I feel that this must be changed. How would it be if you were to send me a little money each month in advance? You would never miss it, while I could shut myself up in my small room and be quite happy. As Matthew said: "Let him who hath two coats give one to the poor." And now I hope that you will listen to the voice which tells you again and again to remember your loving, hoping, poor, and once more I repeat, poor — brother Franz.

Franz hoped that he would not have to wait too long for Ferdinand to answer his letter. He was so hungry most of the time that it was difficult to work with such an empty feeling inside him.

He wished that he had pocket money like the other boys so that he could buy good things to eat from the baker at the end of the street.

One morning after Franz had finished his lesson on the violin, Herr Ruziczka carefully wiped his spectacles and looked at his pupil.

"You have made rapid progress in your music this year, Schubert. Tomorrow you will take the chair of the first violin in the orchestra."

Franz was overjoyed that now, after these many months of hard work, he had at last won the highest place of honor in the orchestra!

"And more than that — when I must be absent, you will take my place and conduct the orchestra."

To lead the orchestra! This was almost too much for Franz to believe.

Just then a knock sounded at the door.

"Yes, yes — come in!" called Herr Ruziczka.

The door opened and the great master, Salieri, came into the room.

"You are here just in time, Herr Salieri. This is our young Franz Schubert who has been composing music. He has learned so fast that I have no more to teach him and now he must begin to work with you."

"Then play some of your compositions for me, Schubert, so that I may see what you have done."

Franz went quietly to the piano and began to play his own music, composing some of it as he went along.

These lovely waltzes that he composed you will surely
enjoy.

THREE WALTZES
(MUSIC APPRECIATION DISC 5 TRACK 48)

Salieri became more and more interested. He walked about the room, listening closely to every note. When Franz stopped playing, he went quickly to the piano.

"My boy, you have been given a great gift — the gift of melody! You must bring your compositions to me very soon and we will go over them carefully," said the master.

To work with the great Salieri! Franz was so excited he could hardly wait for his friend Spaun to visit him that evening, when he could tell him the good news and play his new music for him.

You may be able to play these lively dances that Franz wrote.

GERMAN DANCES
(MUSIC APPRECIATION DISC 5 TRACK 49)

The next day Franz sat in his new place of honor long before it was time, waiting eagerly for the orchestra rehearsal to begin.

When the boys were seated with their instruments ready to play, Herr Ruziczka came into the room and stood ready to conduct.

"From now on, Franz Peter Schubert will lead the first violins. This is the highest honor that can come to anyone in the orchestra. Now then — we will begin with the Beethoven symphony."

Down came the hand of the leader and the music began, every boy watching the director closely. Of all the music that the orchestra played, Franz liked most the compositions of the young Beethoven. He was filled with joy as the beautiful music sounded through the room.

Not many weeks later, a rehearsal was called to practice music in the royal chapel for a special feast day. When the boys had finished playing, the director said:

"You will meet here again tomorrow morning and Franz Schubert will conduct the orchestra."

To lead the orchestra! Franz left the room and from then until the morning he could think of nothing else.

Very early the next day, long before the masters or the boys were awake, Franz went to the music room and seating himself at the director's desk, he carefully studied the music that each instrument was to play and just how the composer meant it to sound.

When the boys came into the room they quickly tuned their instruments and when all was ready, Franz gave the signal to begin. Everyone watched him closely for Franz was serious indeed and thought of nothing but the music and how it should be played.

Many times he stopped the orchestra to go over and over the difficult parts. Never before had there been such a rehearsal. When it was over, the boys crowded around Franz, pounding him on the back and shaking his hand.

"Bravo! Bravo! Schubert!" Their cheers rang through the room.

Franz wanted to shout for joy and he wished that he could always conduct the orchestra.

Whenever he was free he spent his time in the music room teaching himself to play on all the different instruments. In a very short time he played them as easily as if they were toys and now when any boy was absent, he was able to take his place and play on any instrument that was needed.

Franz liked especially to compose merry country dances.
They are called ecossaises.

ECOSSAISES
(MUSIC APPRECIATION DISC 5 TRACK 51)

Franz enjoyed the evenings at the Convict for then his good friends gathered in the music room. After Spaun had arrived, there was music by Stadler, who played some of his own compositions. Then Kenner and Senn read their new poems.

"And what music have you for us this time, Schubert?" asked Spaun.

"I have written something for the orchestra — it is not very much, but perhaps you will all try it with me. You, Spaun, can play the violin part, Holzapfel the cello, Senn the horn, and I will play the other parts on the piano."

The music filled the room and when they had finished, the players rapped loudly on their desks and cried: "Bravo! Bravo!"

Herr Ruziczka heard of the new music that Franz had written and at the orchestra rehearsal the next morning the boys played the new composition, exclaiming with delight after they had heard the beautiful melodies.

"Your music is very good indeed, Franz. We will play it at our concert on Thursday night," said the director.

"Thank you, Herr Ruziczka — this is a great honor that you have given me!" exclaimed Franz.

"The music is worthy of the honor, Schubert," said the director, smiling.

It was a warm summer evening and the windows of the Convict were opened wide before beginning the Thursday night concert.

When the music began, people coming home from the nearby parks stopped outside to listen. Soon there was no room in the narrow street for anyone to pass and from his

small house across from the Convict, jolly Herr Hanacek hurried to bring chairs for the ladies to sit upon.

After the music of Mozart and Beethoven had been played, Franz stood and conducted the boys in his own composition.

When they had finished there was loud applause from the audience outside.

"Play it again! Play that music again!"

Franz was delighted, and from then on, his music was a part of every Thursday night concert.

Perhaps you can play this duet with someone. It is a military march that Schubert wrote and there is still another part that you may want to play as well.

MARCH MILITAIRE - Secondo
(MUSIC APPRECIATION DISC 5 TRACK 53)

MARCH MILITAIRE - Primo
(MUSIC APPRECIATION DISC 5 TRACK 54)

(MUSIC APPRECIATION DISC 5 TRACK 55 is the MARCH MILITAIRE - Primo & Secondo Duet)

72

Franz had been working hard at his studies and now that good reports were again sent to his father, he was allowed to return home on Sunday afternoons.

For Schoolmaster Schubert's birthday he composed some special music and his father was delighted with the new song that his three sons sang to him.

Franz was also allowed to leave the school on special days to go to the home of Salieri to show the master his compositions.

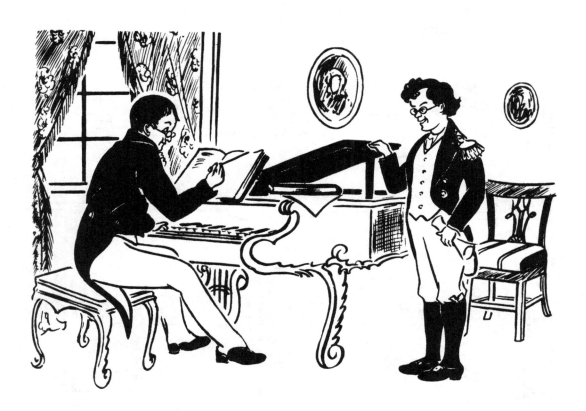

"Yes, Franz — this work is good indeed," said Salieri, going over the compositions one day. "There is not much to change — just a little here and there. Sometime you must try to write an opera."

His pupil did not come again for several weeks. Salieri began to wonder what had happened when Franz suddenly appeared in the doorway with a large roll of music under his arm.

"What is this that you have brought to show me?" asked the master.

Franz stood anxiously waiting while Salieri opened the closely written sheets of music.

"An opera! And finished in this short time! But I cannot believe that such a thing is possible!"

The master looked in wonder at the young man before him.

"You seem to have learned almost everything for yourself, Franz. Indeed there is not much more that I can teach you."

In one of his operas called ROSAMUNDE, Franz wrote this dance music for a ballet.

BALLET FROM ROSAMUNDE
(MUSIC APPRECIATION DISC 5 TRACK 56)

Andantino

For Herr Lange's birthday, Franz composed his first music for an orchestra — the Symphony in D, and the director was happy indeed when it was played at a special celebration in his honor.

And now, after Franz had been at the Convict for five years, his voice was not so high and clear as it had been, so he could no longer sing in the choir.

"If you pass the examinations in mathematics, Schubert, you may stay on with us here in the Convict and play in the orchestra," said the director.

Mathematics! It had been a hard study for Franz and now that it was necessary for him to earn his living, he wondered if it would not be better to leave the Convict and enter the training school where he could learn how to teach the small children in his father's school.

Theodor Schubert was delighted with the news.

"At last, Franz!" he exclaimed. "At last you will become a schoolmaster — like all the Schuberts!"

CHAPTER FOUR

THE FRESH GREEN leaves glistened in the spring sunshine as Franz climbed in the mountains near Vienna early one morning.

He was so glad to be free from the schoolroom and the mischievous children that he began to sing, his voice ringing joyously through the forest. He climbed higher and higher, stopping often to look back at the beautiful countryside below him.

When he came to a little inn at the side of the road he was tired and sat down to rest. He wondered what he could buy to eat with the few coins in his pocket, for he was very hungry.

As Franz walked through the low doorway he saw that the inn was filled with gaily dressed people. But everyone seemed to be unhappy. Even the innkeeper looked as if something had gone wrong.

"Is there anything the matter, sir?" asked Franz.

"Yes, yes — everything is wrong!" cried the innkeeper. "The bridal party has come here to feast and dance, but we have no music, for the village band has been called to play at another tavern."

"Perhaps I can help you," said Franz.

The innkeeper looked at the short, plump young man in steel spectacles and shabby city clothes.

"You? But what could you do?"

"Let me show you, sir," said Franz quietly, as he went to a broken-down piano in one corner of the room.

He sat at the old instrument and played a few chords. Then his fingers ran swiftly over the broken keys and gay melodies began to fill the room.

Everyone looked up in surprise and soon the young peasant folk were gaily dancing and singing.

This German dance that Franz composed is indeed a merry
one.

GERMAN DANCE

(MUSIC APPRECIATION DISC 5 TRACK 57)

Franz played one jolly tune after another and the innkeeper
was overjoyed to see everyone so happy.

"Thank you, my young man. You have served us well this day. Come! You shall have a feast fit for a king," and the happy innkeeper led the young pianist to a table piled high with good things to eat.

It was late when Franz returned to the small dark schoolroom and started to correct the exercise papers so that they would be ready for his young pupils the next morning.

Suddenly he caught sight of a book by the great poet, Goethe. Eagerly turning the pages, he came to the poem, "The

Erlking," that told the story of a father riding on his black horse through a shadowy forest at midnight, in search of a doctor for the sick child held close in his arms.

Franz could hear in his mind the sound of the horse's hoofs as they galloped faster and faster through the night.

He walked rapidly about the room, reading the poem again and again. Then sweeping the pile of copybooks to the floor, he seized music paper and wrote the notes of a song as fast as his pen could travel.

But the music came into his mind faster than he could write, so he began to put down only the bars at the end of the measures, with a few notes here and there so that he would remember how the music was to sound.

In less than an hour the song was finished and looking up, Franz discovered that his friend had come into the room.

"Spaun! But see — I have just finished a song: 'The Erlking.' I must try it on a piano to see how it sounds."

"We will go to the choir school at once!" cried his friend and they ran through the streets to the Convict.

"Come, Stadler and Holzapfel — Franz has just composed some new music!" called Spaun. "Tell Herr Ruziczka to come!"

They gathered about the piano and Franz played the music while Holzapfel sang the voice part.

Everyone became more and more excited as the galloping of the horse's hoofs sounded throughout the accompaniment.

When it was finished, the boys applauded loudly and then Herr Ruziczka played the music over and over.

"Yes — it is indeed a beautiful song — the finest that you have written," said the master.

"It might be — if it were not so difficult to play!" laughed Franz.

The music of "The Erlking" could no longer be kept from the others and soon the room was filled with the masters and the boys who listened in wonder to the song that Franz had written.

Can you hear the galloping of the horse's hoofs in the opening part of the music?

THEME OF ERLKING
(MUSIC APPRECIATION DISC 5 TRACK 58)

Day after day Franz went on with the work that he did not like — teaching children the alphabet, their spelling, and arithmetic, while all the time his mind was filled with music that he wanted to put down on paper.

In the summer time it was hot and stuffy in the crowded room with its low ceiling, for no breeze could find its way through the narrow window. In the winter it was always cold and dark and the children sat with their eyes close to their books, trying to read their lessons in the dim light that came from a small oil lamp.

86

During the morning Franz always found something for them to study, so that he could write his melodies. He forgot everything about him as he filled sheet after sheet with notes.

Spaun brought him music paper whenever he came to visit, for the little money that Theodor Schubert gave his son for teaching in his school was never enough to buy all that he needed.

One beautiful composition after another came from his pen and at the end of a year he had written one hundred fifty songs, a string quartet, symphonies, two piano sonatas and four operas!

This lovely song that he wrote, called "Hedge Roses," you

will want to sing while someone plays it for you.

HEDGE ROSES
(MUSIC APPRECIATION DISC 5 TRACK 59)

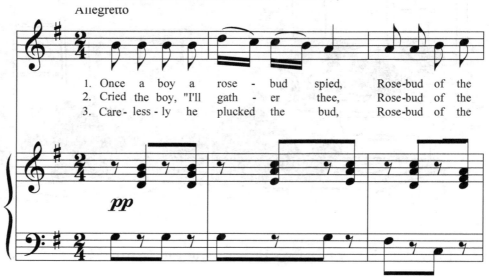

1. Once a boy a rose - bud spied, Rose-bud of the
2. Cried the boy, "I'll gath - er thee, Rose-bud of the
3. Care - less - ly he plucked the bud, Rose-bud of the

wild - wood, Fresh and young and pass - ing fair,
wild - wood," Said the rose, "My thorns you'll see,
wild - wood, Quick she stings, but all in vain,

Swift he ran to see it there, All the air per -
If thou dar'st to in - jure me, I will nev - er
Hear - ing not her cries of pain, Gone her sweet per -

fum - ing. Rose - bud, Rose - bud, Rose - bud red,
bow to thee. Rose - bud, Rose - bud, Rose - bud red,
fum - ing. Rose - bud, Rose - bud, Rose - bud red,

pp

Rose-bud of the wild - wood.
Rose-bud of the wild - wood.
Rose-bud of the wild - wood.

On Sunday afternoons Franz visited his friends Stadler and Holzapfel at the Convict. Spaun, too, was often with them and together they played and sang Franz's new music that he brought with him.

When the boys had to leave to sing for the late afternoon service in the chapel, Stadler took Franz to the study room.

"Here is a book of poems that you may want to read while we go to sing in the choir," he said, with a twinkle in his eye. He pushed Franz into the room, locked the door after him and put the key in his pocket.

"Be sure to have some music written for us when we come back for you," Stadler called gaily as he ran down the hall.

But Franz did not mind being locked in, for he was always happiest when he was composing. After the service, when the boys came for him again, he had several beautiful songs ready for them.

"You may have them all to keep, if you like them," said Franz, smiling.

Every evening he took his new music for Salieri to see.

The master was very fond of his pupil and spent long hours with him.

"There is soon to be a celebration in the Lichtenthal parish church, Franz. Why do you not take the composition that you have just written and conduct it yourself at the special service?"

Franz was delighted and directed the many rehearsals that were held in the church.

When the night arrived, he stood to lead the chorus and felt very uncomfortable in his new coat. His neck was hidden in a large white collar held up by a big black tie.

All his good friends were there and they were proud and delighted as they listened to the beautiful music of the mass that he had written.

Salieri, the great master, was seated in the audience, and when the celebration was over, he hurried to Franz.

"I am happy to call you my pupil!" he cried. "You will indeed bring me much honor."

Not long afterward Spaun brought his friend Schober to the schoolroom to meet Franz.

"So you are Schubert! I have often heard your songs at the home of Spaun and have brought you a poem that our friend Mayerhofer has just written. I thought that you might like to read it," said Schober, handing the poem to Franz.

"It is beautiful — yes, very beautiful!" said Franz, after he had read the lines.

In a moment he had forgotten his visitors and was already setting the verse to music. Spaun and Schober left the room quietly and in a few hours the song was finished.

Franz took the sheets of music that were still wet with ink and ran with them to the house of Spaun where he found the young Schober.

"Here is the music," he called. "Perhaps your friend Mayerhofer would like to see his poem in a song."

"But surely you have not finished it so soon!" cried Schober, looking in astonishment at the sheets of music. "I must take it to Mayerhofer at once!" he exclaimed as he hurried off to find the poet.

From now on Schober spent all of his spare moments in the schoolroom with Franz and the two became good friends.

Night after night he found Franz bent over the copybooks of his pupils in the dim light. There were always sheets of freshly written music scattered over the floor.

"Why do you stay here in this room doing work that you so dislike, when all of your time should be spent in writing music?" asked his friend.

"What else is there for me to do?" answered Franz, sadly. "I must earn my living, and music will not do that for me now."

Suddenly a smile lighted Schober's face.

"I have it!" he cried. "You shall come to live with me — now — at once!"

"But my father — what would he say?"

"We will go and find him. Hurry, Franz!" exclaimed his friend, gathering up the music papers and putting them under his arm.

They left the room where Franz had struggled to teach unruly children for three long years and found Theodor Schubert in the next room at his desk.

The schoolmaster looked severely at his son when he heard of the new plan.

"You are making a foolish mistake, Franz, and remember that from now on you can expect no help from me. You will be back again to teach, no doubt, for you know that you will have to earn your own living."

Schober helped Franz gather his few belongings together and soon they were on their way down the street. It was late when they climbed the stairs to the small room which they shared for the next few months.

Schober saw that Franz had food and clothing while Spaun and Stadler kept him supplied with music paper.

"We have great news for you, Schubert!" cried his friends after Franz had returned one day from giving music lessons to pupils that his friends had found for him. "Count Esterhazy wishes you to teach music to his children."

"The great Count Esterhazy?"

"Yes, and better still, he wishes you to go with his family to live at his summer home in Hungary!"

"Then I must see the count at once to find out when they will be ready to leave," said Franz.

Soon he had moved to the Esterhazy home in the country and was living in the servants' quarters. Each day there were lessons in music to give to the three children of the count, but the rest of the time Franz was free to do as he wished.

He went for long walks over the beautiful countryside
and enjoyed the singing and dancing of the gypsy folk who
wandered carefree from place to place.

Franz thought often of his friends in Vienna and his home
in Lichtenthal and sat down to write a letter to his brother.

24th August, 1818

Dear Ferdinand,

It is half past eleven at night, and I have just finished your music — the "Requiem." My foot has gone to sleep and that is very annoying. If the silly thing could write, it wouldn't fall asleep. — Good morning, little brother! I fell asleep as well as my foot and am now continuing this letter on the 25th, at eight o'clock in the morning. Give greetings to my dear parents, brothers, sisters, friends, and acquaintances. Tell mother that my linen is well looked after and that I am happy that she thinks of me. Of course if there is an extra supply, I would be very pleased if you could send me some handkerchiefs, neckscarves and stockings. I badly need two pairs of cashmere trousers as well. I would send money for them at once.

It is beginning to be cold here, but we shall not set out for Vienna before the middle of November. The harvest here is very interesting. The corn is not gathered as in Austria, but is stacked in the open fields in what they call "Tristen." They are built so skillfully that the rain runs off them without doing any damage. In spite of everything going well and my health being good, and the people here being so kind, I am counting the days till the word goes forth: To Vienna! To Vienna! Yes, beloved Vienna, you hold the dearest and most precious things in my life, and nothing but the blessed sight of them again will make me happy.

I remain with love to all
Your true and faithful Franz.

The first snow had spread a thick carpet on the ground when Franz returned to Vienna. Everyone was delighted to have him back again and his friends had planned many celebrations for his home-coming.

They went from one inn to another, feasting, singing and playing on their instruments until late into the night. On their way home there were snow battles with Stadler, Holzapfel, and Schober hiding behind umbrellas while Spaun, Mayerhofer, and Franz rushed at them and pelted them with snow.

Then stealing quietly to nearby houses, they rang the doorbells and ran swiftly to hide in alley-ways and behind trees so that they could watch nightcaps appear at windows and doors to see who was calling at this hour of the night.

When Theodor Schubert heard that his son was again in Vienna, he asked him to return to the school, but Franz had already gone to live with Mayerhofer.

Before leaving for his work each morning, the poet sat at the table in the dark gloomy room with its tumbledown furniture, writing one lovely verse after another, talking to himself as he worked.

As soon as they were finished, Franz reached across the table for the poems to set them to music, and hummed the melodies so that he would not hear the loud mumblings of his friend.

"Ah, Schubert — I like my poems so much better after you have set them to music!" exclaimed Mayerhofer as he listened to the lovely songs that Franz played on the old rickety piano.

When it was time for him to leave for his work across the city, Mayerhofer dressed in whatever clothing he could find about the room, leaving Franz to wear what was left when he was ready to go to the Esterhazy home in Vienna.

After the lessons were finished, Franz enjoyed walking

alone in the country. But when evening came he liked to go to the coffeehouses with his jolly companions. Often he took his new compositions to play for them.

His merry friends liked to listen to the delightful music that he wrote. This "Moment Musicale" you will want to hear many times.

MOMENT MUSICALE
(MUSIC APPRECIATION DISC 5 TRACK 60)
Allegro moderato

One afternoon Schober brought his friend Vogl, the greatest singer in all Vienna, to see Schubert. They found him seated at the table, busily writing.

Vogl looked about the untidy room with clothing lying over the broken furniture and music scattered on the floor.

"Are these all your songs?" asked the tall singer, pointing to a great pile of music on the chair.

"Yes, and there is still much more in the cupboard."

"How do you find time to write so much music?" asked Vogl.

"Whenever I finish one thing, I begin another," answered Franz.

"But your glasses are bent — do they not bother you when you write your music?"

"Yes — but you see, I wear them to bed to save time looking for them when I get up in the morning," explained Franz.

Vogl laughed heartily. "Schober would not rest until I came to see your songs. But I could never sing them all! May I take some of them with me to look over?"

"Oh, yes — as many as you wish, and I will write more of them," answered Franz.

In a few days Vogl was back at Mayerhofer's room.

"But see here, Schubert — your music is very good. Why, I cannot get enough of this 'Erlking' of yours. Come — play for me while I sing it."

Soon his beautiful voice rang through the little room.

"Again! I must sing it again!" cried Vogl, and once more the music echoed through the house, the clattering hoof-beats sounding in the accompaniment.

And now Vogl spent a part of each morning with Franz, going over his new songs. He sang many of them in concerts for the people of Vienna.

Often the great singer took Franz to the Austrian mountains for short vacations where the days were spent in tramping through the forest. In the evenings there were musical gatherings at the homes of Vogl's many friends, who were delighted with Franz's music that was played and sung for them.

Even though he enjoyed these happy days, Franz was always glad to go back to his beloved Vienna.

One day after he returned from the mountains, he found a small sum of money that had just been sent to him for one of his compositions. He was overjoyed with his good fortune and rushed about to tell his friends.

"We will have a big celebration tonight! You must all come to the inn for a feast, for money is as thick as blackberries with me now!" he cried and hurried away to see that all would be ready for the evening.

When the hour arrived, Franz met his friends at the door of the inn, his tight curly hair standing on end, his face beaming with joy. He was never so happy as when he could entertain his companions.

And now Franz moved to a large house just outside Vienna. There were noted writers, musicians and artists living in the old house and Franz was delighted to be in such noble company.

All that one had to do if one needed clothing was to go to a friend's room and find boots, a cravat, or a coat to wear. Whoever had money paid for the meals for the day or an evening's entertainment at an inn.

On warm summer evenings, Franz's compositions were played in the parks nearby and people came from far and near to listen to his music.

Every afternoon Franz and his friends walked through the beautiful forest behind the old house. One day, after tramping along the pathways they sat down to rest at a tavern. Schober took a book of verses from his pocket by the poet Shakespeare and began to read the lines: "Hark! Hark! the lark at heaven's gate sings."

Franz listened eagerly to the beautiful poem.

"Oh, such a lovely melody has just come into my mind!" he cried. "If only I had some music paper!"

"Here — why not use this," said Schober, quickly drawing some lines on the back of a menu card.

Franz seized a pen and hearing nothing of the noise and laughter about him, set the words to music on the back of the card.

Before his friends had finished their coffee, he handed them the new song, its joyous melody, like the song of the lark, rising and falling and soaring upward again in his beautiful: "Hark! Hark! the Lark."

HARK! HARK! THE LARK
(MUSIC APPRECIATION DISC 5 TRACK 61)

Allegretto

Hark! hark! the lark at heaven's gate sings, And Phoe - bus 'gins to

"What a lovely song, Franz!" said Stadler, softly humming the new music.

"Ah, but sometime I hope I may write something really fine, like the composer Beethoven. No one has ever written greater music than he."

"Your music is very beautiful, too," said Spaun.

But Franz had not heard him. He sat thinking for a moment. Then turning suddenly to Spaun, he asked eagerly:

"Do you think that the great Beethoven would look at my compositions and tell me if there is hope for my music?"

"Why not go to see him, Franz? Surely it would do no harm," answered Spaun, kindly.

That very afternoon Franz took some of his compositions from a cupboard and across the top of them he wrote: "To Beethoven." Rolling them into a small bundle, he put them under his arm and hurried to the house of the great master.

A servant opened the door to find a short, very frightened young man in spectacles.

"Here!" gasped Franz, pushing the music into his hands. "Give this to your master!" and rushing from the doorway, he ran down the street and did not stop until he was back in his room again.

The next evening there was an entertainment in Schubert's honor to celebrate the printing of "The Erlking," for at last his friends had gathered together their small earnings to have it published.

Vogl sang the beautiful song while Franz played the accompaniment. There was a burst of applause when the music was finished and Franz was very happy because his friends liked his song.

A few days later he came home to find his friend Hüttenbrenner waiting for him.

"We must go at once to the theater, Schubert! At last they are giving one of your operas and Vogl is singing the leading part. I have promised that you will be there to hear him."

They went quickly to the theater where the lights were already lowered for the performance.

Franz leaned forward and listened to his music as though he had never heard it before. He was proud of his friend Vogl, whose powerful voice rang through the theater.

There was loud applause when the curtain went down. Vogl came onto the stage again to speak to the people.

"Ladies and gentlemen — I believe that you would like to see the composer who has written this delightful music. Will Franz Peter Schubert come to the stage?"

Franz clutched the arm of Hüttenbrenner.

"I could not go like this!" he whispered, looking down at his shabby clothes.

"Here, Franz!" cried his friend, pulling off his evening coat. "Put this on — quickly!"

"No! No! I could not do that! Come — we must go at once!" and in the darkness as they stole quietly to the door, they heard Vogl's voice again:

"I am very sorry but Franz Schubert does not seem to be in the audience tonight. Perhaps he will be with us at the next performance of his opera."

But Franz was so busy that he did not even know that the performances were soon ended. He was hard at work composing music for some young people of Vienna who had asked him to write a symphony especially for them.

He felt honored that they wished to play his music in their small orchestra and in a short time he had finished the first two movements of a symphony.

He sat humming the melodies that he had written, drumming on the table with his hand.

"Where are you, Schubert?" called voices outside his door.

"We are leaving for a picnic at once."

"A picnic! Wait! I will come, too! I could not miss a picnic with my good friends!" and pushing the music into a drawer, he rushed out, and never again remembered to finish his symphony.

This melody from the "Unfinished Symphony" of Schubert's is one of the most beautiful that he ever wrote.

(MUSIC APPRECIATION DISC 5 TRACK 62)

Allegro

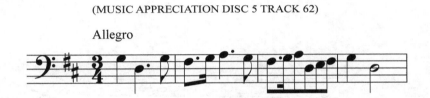

The Hedgehog Inn was now the meeting place for all of Schubert's friends, for here, above the noise and bustle of the busy inn, he had come to live with his old friend Schober.

But the merriment of the people below him did not bother Schubert and he went on composing every morning.

In these past years he had written many compositions for the piano, some symphonies, quartets, sonatas, and over six hundred songs!

Early one evening Franz was returning to the inn after a visit to his brother Ferdinand. As he was going up the narrow stairs he heard strange noises coming from his room. Whatever could they be moving? The sounds grew louder as he climbed the stairs.

Suddenly his door was opened and there in the middle of the room stood a beautiful new piano!

"A tune, Schubert! Play for us!" cried his friends, pushing him to the new instrument.

Before he could ask where the piano had come from, everyone had started a merry dance around him while Franz played a jolly melody.

When it was ended there were loud cheers and stamping of feet.

"But the instrument — where did it come from?" asked Franz.

"It is yours!" cried Spaun. "You will no longer need to go about searching for a piano to try your compositions when you have finished them."

"But, my friends — you have done this for me?" exclaimed Franz, running his fingers softly over the keys.

"You have given us more joy with your music, Franz, than you will ever know," said Schober.

"And now, what is this music on the floor?" asked Stadler, picking up the scattered sheets.

"It is a theme from an impromptu," said Schubert. "Here — I will play it for you."

THEME FROM IMPROMPTU
(MUSIC APPRECIATION DISC 5 TRACK 63)

 Late into the night they sat listening to their beloved Franz as he played his beautiful music and when the good friends left to go to their homes, Schubert leaned from his open window to watch them below.

He shook his head and smiled. "My merry, faithful friends! What would I ever do without them!"

He could hear them singing his melodies as they went down the narrow, dimly lighted streets of Vienna.

And his melodies are still giving joy to all the world — the beautiful singing melodies of Franz Peter Schubert.

Franz Schubert and His Merry Friends is part of *Music Appreciation for the Elementary Grade: Book 1.*

Music Appreciation for the Elementary Grades will introduce children to seven different composers, dating from 1685 to 1828 (Bach, Handel, Haydn, Mozart, Beethoven, Paganini and Schubert). Each composer's childhood and adult life are vividly described in individual biographies. Every important incident is mentioned and every detail of the stories is true. Each book contains written music and delightful pictures throughout. It is more than the human side of these books that will make them live, for in the music the great masters breathe.

The Student Activity book includes a variety of hands-on activities such as: geography lessons, history lessons, recipes, instrument studies, music vocabulary, hand writing, musical facts of the Classical period, timelines, character trait studies, and so much more. Geared for a variety of learners—auditory, kinesthetic, visual, and just plain "active"—the Student Activity Book is an excellent companion to your reading experience.

<u>*Titles used in this curriculum are:*</u>
Sebastian Bach, The Boy from Thuringia
Handel at the Court of Kings
Joseph Haydn, The Merry Little Peasant
Mozart, The Wonder Boy
Ludwig Beethoven and the Chiming Tower Bells
Paganini, Master of Strings
Franz Schubert and His Merry Friends

For more information visit our website at www.Zeezok.com

CPSIA information can be obtained
at www.ICGtesting.com
Printed in the USA
BVHW090448190821
614520BV00005B/355